Intermediate AI
Understanding More About How AI Works

By
Dr. Edward K. S. Buckman, PhD, MBCI, CBCP, ITIL

Illustrations and Learning Design by
Nexora AI Learning Lab

Published by
Nexora Press

First Edition – 2025

Explore the Nexora Press Learning Series

At Nexora Press, we believe learning is a journey, one that grows as your knowledge grows. That's why we've created two connected book series that work together to help young minds explore the world of Artificial Intelligence and Coding.

AI Learning Series

- *Fundamentals of AI for Young Minds* (Ages 7–12)
- *Intermediate AI: Understanding More About How AI Works* (Ages 10–14)
- *Advanced AI* (Coming Soon)

Coding for Young Minds Series

- *Coding for Young Minds* (Ages 8–12)
- *Intermediate Code* (Ages 12–16)
- *Advanced Code* (Coming Soon)

Whether you're curious about smart machines or ready to start coding your own programs, these books will guide you step-by-step.

Learn more at: www.nexorapress.com

Publishing Information

Title: *Intermediate AI — Understanding More About How AI Works*
Author: Dr. Edward Kofi Sasa Buckman
Publisher: Nexora Press
Year of Publication: 2025
ISBN: 979-8-9991843-1-3
Edition: First Edition
Version: 1.0
Printing Location: Printed in the United States of America
Publisher Contact:
Nexora Press
1003 Division Street
Johnson City, TN 37601
Email: info@nexorapress.com
Website: www.nexorapress.com

Legal & Copyright Information

This book is a work of educational nonfiction. While every effort has been made to ensure accuracy, the author and publisher make no guarantees and assume no responsibility for errors or omissions. The content is for informational purposes only and not intended as technical or legal advice.

Copyright Disclaimer

This work is a human-authored creation developed with the assistance of artificial intelligence tools. While some visual and textual elements were generated using AI, the author was responsible for the concept, structure, editing, creative direction, and final composition.

Dedication Page

To the curious minds who never stop asking "Why?"
This book is for you: the future scientists, inventors, and thinkers who will shape tomorrow's world.

Preface

Welcome to Intermediate AI!

In this second book of the Nexora Press AI Learning Series, we will go beyond the basics and dig deeper into how AI works inside. You'll discover how data helps machines make decisions, how neural networks are modeled after the brain, and how AI can sometimes get things wrong.

Just like the first book, you'll still find:

- Fun explanations
- Activities you can try at home or in class
- Vocabulary that makes big ideas easy to understand

Whether you're a student, parent, or teacher, this book is designed to build your confidence in understanding AI and prepare you for even bigger learning ahead.

Let's continue this exciting AI journey together!

The Author

Dr. Edward Kofi Sasa Buckman is an educator, technologist, and passionate advocate for AI literacy. With deep expertise in cybersecurity, risk management, and artificial intelligence, Dr. Buckman's mission is to simplify complex topics and empower young learners to become responsible creators and users of future technologies.

Through the Nexora Press AI Learning Series, Dr. Buckman hopes to inspire the next generation of innovators who will use technology ethically, creatively, and wisely.

Table of Contents

Chapter 1: How Machines Learn

Objectives:

- Understand the core types of machine learning
- Identify how different learning methods are used in real-world AI applications
- Lay the foundation for deeper AI concepts

Introduction

Artificial Intelligence (AI) systems learn using **data**. Unlike humans, who learn from experiences, conversations, or instructions, machines learn from **patterns in large data sets**.

This process is called **Machine Learning**, a branch of AI that allows machines to improve performance over time **without being explicitly programmed**.

The Three Main Types of Machine Learning

1. Supervised Learning

In supervised learning, the machine is trained with a labeled dataset, that is, data that includes both the input and the correct output.

- **Example:** A dataset with images of animals, labeled "dog" or "cat."
- The machine uses these examples to learn how to classify new, unseen images.

Common Use Cases:

- Spam email detection
- Voice recognition
- Image classification

2. Unsupervised Learning

Here, the machine is given data **without labels** and must find patterns or structure in the data.

- **Example:** Grouping customers into clusters based on buying habits.
- The machine discovers similarities on its own.

Common Use Cases:

- Market segmentation
- Recommendation systems
- Anomaly detection (e.g., fraud detection)

3. Reinforcement Learning

This type of learning mimics the way humans learn through trial and error. The AI receives rewards for good actions and penalties for mistakes.

- **Example:** Teaching a robot to walk or an AI to play video games.
- The system learns to maximize reward through repeated trials.

Common Use Cases:

- Game playing (e.g., AlphaGo)
- Self-driving vehicles
- Robotics

How Machines Improve

Each learning method involves an algorithm that adjusts itself based on **feedback or data**. Over time, performance improves as the model **generalizes patterns** from the training data.

Tip: Machine learning isn't about memorizing answers, it's about learning patterns to predict outcomes.

Key Terms

Term	Definition
Algorithm	A set of rules or steps the machine follows to learn from data
Model	The result of training an AI system using data
Training Data	Data used to teach the machine
Accuracy	How well the model predicts or classifies correctly

Quick Review

- Machine learning allows AI systems to learn from data.
- There are three primary learning types: Supervised, Unsupervised, and Reinforcement.
- Each type is suited to different real-world problems.

Chapter 2: Neural Networks – The Brains Behind AI

Objectives:

- Understand what a neural network is
- Learn how neural networks mimic the human brain
- Explore where and how neural networks are used

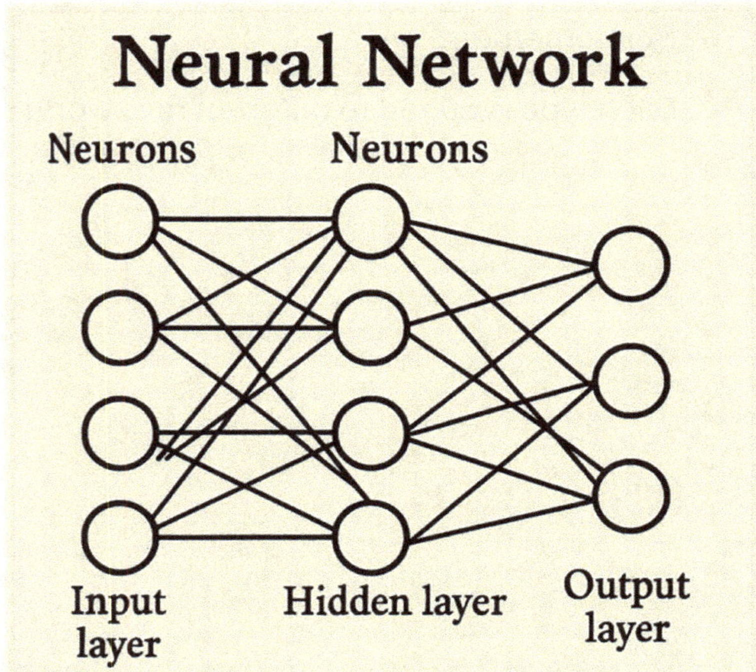

Neurons in a neural network are associated nodes that process data in layers.

What Are Neural Networks?

At the core of many modern AI systems lies a powerful concept called the **neural network**. Inspired by the **structure of the human brain**, neural networks are a series of **connected nodes (called neurons)** that process data in layers.

Think of a neural network like a **network of switches** that turn on and off to process information and make decisions.

Basic Structure of a Neural Network

A typical neural network consists of **three types of layers**:

1. **Input Layer**: Takes in the raw data (like an image or a sentence).
2. **Hidden Layers**: These layers do the actual processing through weighted connections.
3. **Output Layer**: Produces the final result (like a label: “cat” or “dog”).

Each **neuron** in one layer is connected to neurons in the next layer, and each connection has a **weight**, a number that tells the network how important that connection is.

How Does a Neural Network Learn?

Neural networks learn by adjusting their weights during training. Here's a simplified breakdown:

1. **Forward Pass**: The input is passed through the layers to get a prediction.
2. **Loss Calculation**: The model checks how far off the prediction was from the correct answer.
3. **Backward Pass (Backpropagation)**: The model adjusts the weights to reduce future errors.

This process happens **thousands or even millions of times** during training.

Why Are Neural Networks Powerful?

Neural networks can:

- **Recognize images and speech**
- **Translate languages**
- **Play complex games**
- **Drive autonomous cars**

They are **flexible and scalable**, meaning they can be designed to handle everything from basic classification tasks to real-time decision-making systems.

Deep Learning

When a neural network has **many hidden layers**, it is called a **deep neural network**, and the process of training it is called **deep learning**.

Deep learning is the technology behind:

- **Facial recognition**
- **Virtual assistants**
- **Language models** like ChatGPT

Key Terms

Term	**Definition**
Neuron	A node in the network that processes input and sends output
Weight	A value that adjusts the strength of a connection
Layer	A group of neurons that work together
Backpropagation	A method for updating weights to improve learning
Deep Learning	Training very large, multi-layered neural networks

Quick Review

- Neural networks are inspired by the human brain and consist of layers of neurons.
- Learning happens by adjusting weights using algorithms like backpropagation.
- Deep learning enables complex AI applications in vision, speech, and language.

Chapter 3: Real-World Applications of Neural Networks

Objectives:

- Explore how neural networks are used in real-world scenarios
- Understand the impact of AI across different industries
- Connect neural network concepts with daily life and careers

1. Healthcare: Diagnosing Diseases

Neural networks are trained on thousands of medical images, like X-rays or MRIs, to identify patterns of disease that even experienced doctors might miss.

Example: A deep learning model can detect **early-stage cancer** or **diabetic retinopathy** by analyzing images pixel by pixel.

Impact: Faster, more accurate diagnoses can save lives and reduce healthcare costs.

2. Gaming: Smarter NPCs and Realistic Graphics

Modern video games use neural networks to create more **realistic characters** and smarter **non-player characters (NPCs)** that adapt to your actions.

Example: AI-powered enemies in games like *The Last of Us Part II* adjust their behavior based on your strategy.

Impact: More immersive and dynamic gaming experiences.

3. Self-Driving Cars

Self-driving cars use **convolutional neural networks (CNNs)** to interpret live camera feeds and recognize stop signs, pedestrians, lane markings, and other vehicles.

Example: Tesla's Autopilot and Waymo's autonomous cars process enormous amounts of sensor data in real-time.

Impact: Safer transportation, reduced human error, and potential mobility for people who cannot drive.

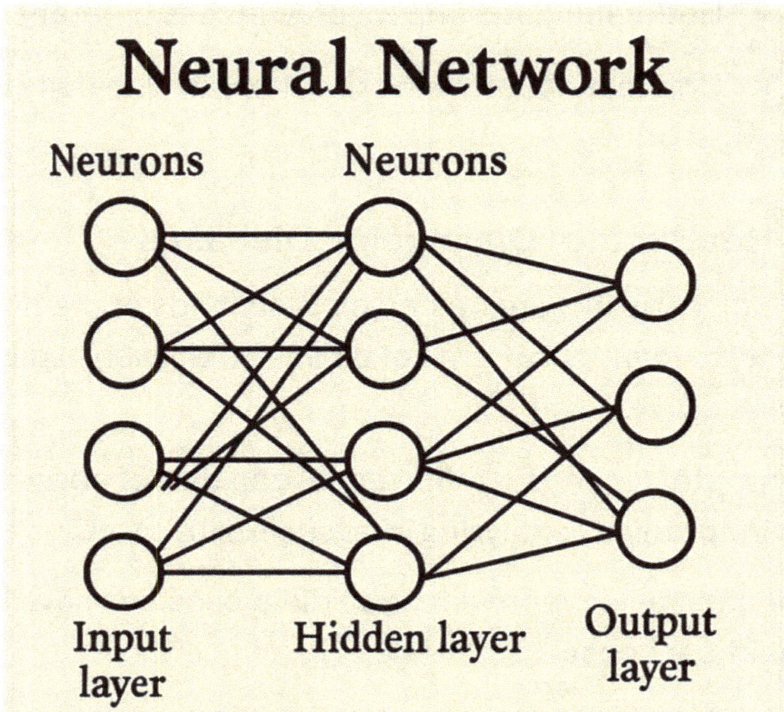

Neurons in a neural network are associa-ted nodes that process data in layers.

4. E-Commerce: Recommendations and Personalization

When you shop online, neural networks analyze your behavior to recommend products you might like.

Example: Amazon or Netflix uses neural networks to suggest products and movies based on your past purchasing and viewing habits.

Impact: Boosts sales and improves customer experience.

5. Language Translation and Chatbots

Neural networks help translate languages in real-time and power conversational AI systems.

Example: Google Translate uses **sequence-to-sequence neural networks** to translate whole sentences, maintaining grammar and context.

Impact: Breaks language barriers and powers customer service chatbots.

6. Art and Creativity

AI can generate art, music, and poetry using **generative neural networks**.

Example: DALL·E creates images from text descriptions. Neural networks like Jukebox generate music in different styles.

Impact: Opens new frontiers in digital creativity and collaboration.

7. Scientific Discovery

Neural networks are used in research to make discoveries faster.

Example: AI helped discover new antibiotics by analyzing molecular structures and predicting their effectiveness.

Impact: Accelerates innovation in medicine, materials, and climate science.

Summary

Neural networks are not just a theory; they're everywhere:

- Diagnosing diseases
- Driving cars
- Translating languages
- Recommending content
- Creating art
- Powering virtual assistants

As AI continues to evolve, neural networks will increasingly play a significant role in shaping how we live, work, and learn.

Reflective Questions

- Which application of neural networks do you find most exciting?
- How might neural networks impact your future career?
- Are there any risks you think we should consider with these technologies?

Chapter 4: AI Training – Data, Bias, and Fairness

Objectives:

- Understand how data is used to train AI models
- Learn what bias in AI means and why it matters
- Explore ways to make AI more fair and trustworthy

1. How AI Learns from Data

Every AI system needs data, lots of it. Neural networks don't "think" the way humans do. Instead, they:

1. **Collect** thousands or millions of examples (like images or sentences),
2. **Detect patterns** in that data,
3. **Make predictions** based on what they've learned.

Example: To train a cat detector, an AI is shown thousands of labeled cat and non-cat photos. It eventually learns what a "cat" looks like, based on patterns of pixels.

2. Training, Validation, Testing

AI training happens in stages:

- **Training set**: Where the model learns.
- **Validation set**: Helps fine-tune the model.
- **Testing set**: Measures how well it performs on unseen data.

If a model does great on training but badly on testing, it's likely **overfitting**—memorizing examples instead of learning general patterns.

3. Bias in AI

Bias in AI occurs when the training data reflects unfair or unbalanced patterns from the real world.

Example: If a facial recognition AI is trained mostly on light-skinned faces, it may perform poorly on darker-skinned ones. This is **racial bias**, and it can lead to real-world harm.

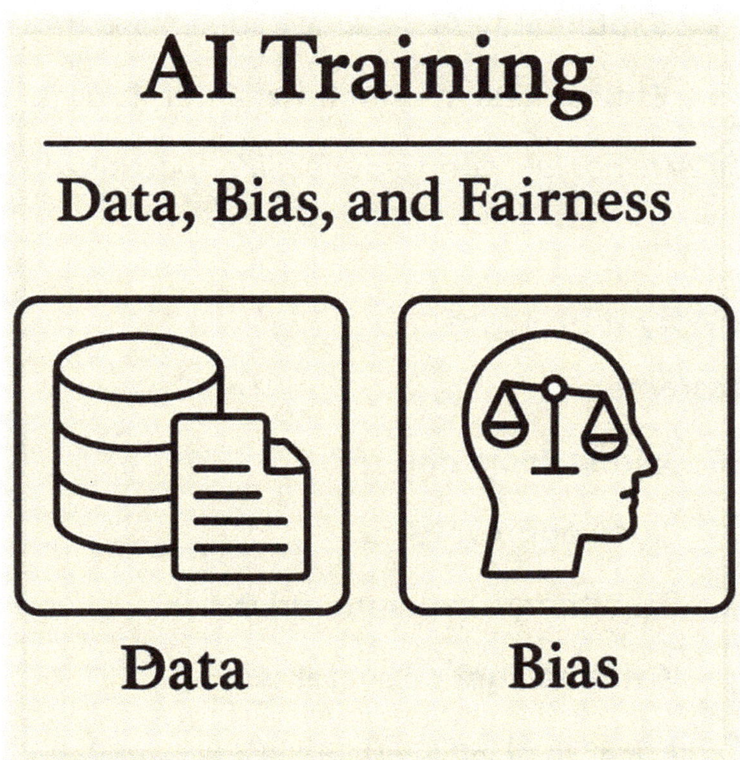

Other examples:

- Gender bias in hiring AIs
- Cultural bias in language models
- Geographic bias in recommendation systems

4. Why Bias Happens

- **Imbalanced data**: Some groups are underrepresented.
- **Human labeling errors**: Mistakes in categorizing data.
- **Hidden assumptions**: Developers may unknowingly embed stereotypes into models.

5. Building Fairer AI

AI developers and researchers work on several methods to reduce bias:

Examples:

- **Diversifying training data**: Including examples from different groups and contexts.
- **Auditing algorithms**: Testing for bias before release.
- **Explainable AI**: Making AI decisions transparent to users.
- **Ethical design principles**: Prioritizing fairness, privacy, and inclusion.

Fair AI is not just good science, it's good citizenship.

6. Why It Matters

AI affects:

- **Hiring decisions**
- **Loan approvals**
- **Healthcare recommendations**
- **Criminal justice systems**

So, fairness in AI isn't a luxury; it's a responsibility.

Summary

- AI learns from data, but flawed data leads to flawed AI.
- Bias is a serious issue that can harm people and worsen inequality.
- Developers must design and test AI carefully to ensure fairness and transparency.

Reflective Questions

- Have you seen examples of bias in technology or media?
- What's one step you think AI developers should take to build fairer systems?
- Would you trust an AI that makes life-impacting decisions? Why or why not?

Chapter 5: Inside a Machine Learning Project – From Data to Deployment

Objectives:

- Understand the key stages of building an AI/ML solution
- Learn what professionals do in each stage
- See how AI moves from an idea to real-world use

1. Problem Definition: What Are We Solving?

Every ML project starts with a **clear goal**.

Examples:

- Predict whether an email is spam
- Detect pneumonia in X-ray images
- Recommend new movies to a user

This is usually phrased as a **prediction problem**, like:

"Given input A, can we predict output B?"

Stakeholders define **success criteria**, like 90% accuracy or reducing manual work.

2. Collecting and Preparing Data

Once the problem is defined, the next step is **data collection**:

- From internal databases (e.g., sales records)
- Public sources (e.g., weather or traffic data)
- APIs or sensor streams

Then, the data is **cleaned and labeled**:

Example:

- Remove duplicates or missing values
- Normalize formats (e.g., dates, currencies)
- Annotate (e.g., marking spam/not spam)

This stage can take **50–80%** of the total project time!

3. Choosing and Training the Model

Next comes **model selection**: What type of ML algorithm will work best?
Common types:

- **Decision Trees**
- **Support Vector Machines**
- **Neural Networks**

Training involves:

- Feeding the model with labeled data
- Adjusting parameters (weights) to reduce prediction errors
- Using tools like TensorFlow or PyTorch

Developers use **training**, **validation**, and **testing** datasets to ensure the model generalizes well.

4. Evaluating the Model

Key metrics used:

- **Accuracy**: How many predictions were correct?

- **Precision & Recall:** Especially important for medical or safety-critical AI.
- **Confusion Matrix:** Helps visualize model performance.

If results are poor:

- Gather more data
- Tune parameters (hyperparameter optimization)
- Try a different model

5. Deployment: Putting AI into the Real World

Once the model performs well, it is **deployed** and integrated into:

- Web apps
- Mobile apps
- IoT devices
- Back-end systems

This involves software engineering tasks:

- Creating APIs
- Ensuring scalability and speed
- Monitoring performance (e.g., "model drift" when the world changes)

6. Iteration and Feedback

Machine Learning projects are never really "done." Models must:

- Be updated regularly
- Be retrained with fresh data
- Be monitored for errors or bias

A model that worked in 2023 might fail in 2025 if user behavior changes!

7. Team Roles in an ML Project

- **Data Scientists**: Build and test models
- **Machine Learning Engineers**: Turn models into production-ready systems
- **Data Engineers**: Manage pipelines and infrastructure
- **Product Managers**: Align goals with business needs
- **Ethics & Compliance Teams**: Ensure responsible AI use

Summary

- Every Machine Learning project follows a pipeline: define problem → gather data → train model → deploy → monitor.
- Real-world Machine Learning requires both data science and engineering skills.
- Success depends on constant iteration and ethical considerations.

Reflective Questions

1. Which step in the ML project lifecycle do you think is most important? Why?
2. What might go wrong if data is bad or biased?
3. Can you think of a real-world app that might be using this pipeline?

Chapter 6: Introduction to Natural Language Processing (NLP)

Objectives:

- Understand what NLP is and why it's important
- Explore how computers process human language
- Learn about common NLP tasks and real-world applications

1. What Is NLP?

Natural Language Processing (NLP) is a field of AI that focuses on enabling machines to understand, interpret, and generate human language.

Simply put, NLP helps computers "read" and "talk" like people do.

It's how Siri understands your voice, how Google Translate works, and how chatbots respond in real-time.

2. The Core Challenges of NLP

Unlike numbers or images, **language is messy**:

- Words can have **multiple meanings** (e.g., "bat" = animal or sports tool)
- Sentences can be **ambiguous** ("He saw the man with the telescope")
- **Grammar and slang** vary across regions and cultures

NLP helps untangle these complexities using algorithms, statistics, and deep learning.

3. Common NLP Tasks

Here are the core functions NLP systems perform:

Task	What It Does	Example
Tokenization	Breaks text into words/sentences	"Hello world" → ["Hello", "world"]
Part-of-Speech Tagging	Identifies nouns, verbs, adjectives, etc.	"run" = noun or verb?
Named Entity Recognition (NER)	Finds people, places, dates	"John visited Paris in April."
Sentiment Analysis	Understands emotion or opinion	"This product is amazing!" = Positive
Text Classification	Categorizes text	Email = spam or not spam
Machine Translation	Converts text between languages	English → French
Text Generation	Produces new text	ChatGPT writing a story

4. How Does NLP Work?

Traditional NLP used **rules and statistical models**, but modern NLP relies on **machine learning and deep learning**, especially:

- **Recurrent Neural Networks (RNNs)**
- **Transformers** like BERT and GPT

Transformers revolutionized NLP by allowing models to "pay attention" to context in a sentence, not just process words one by one.

5. Real-World NLP Applications

Application	How NLP Helps
Chatbots	Understand questions, provide answers
Search Engines	Understand intent and match results
Social Media Monitoring	Detect sentiment or misinformation
Voice Assistants	Convert speech to commands
Document Summarization	Turn long text into key points

6. Ethics and Bias in NLP

NLP models learn from large datasets, often scraped from the internet. This introduces risks:

- **Bias** in gender, race, or culture
- **Misinformation** reproduction
- **Privacy** concerns in chat or voice data

Designing **responsible NLP** means choosing good data, testing for bias, and being transparent.

7. Limitations of NLP

Despite significant progress, NLP is still limited in:

- Understanding sarcasm
- Detecting lies
- Deep emotional nuance

Human language is complex, and sometimes only humans can fully grasp meaning in context.

Summary

- NLP is how machines understand and use human language
- Key tasks include translation, classification, summarization, and sentiment analysis
- Modern NLP uses deep learning models like transformers
- NLP has powerful applications—but also ethical challenges

Reflective Questions

1. How do you use NLP tools in your daily life?
2. Why is context important in understanding language?
3. How could NLP be improved to understand humans better?

Chapter 7: Building an AI Chatbot – A Step-by-Step Project

Objectives:

- Understand how chatbots work
- Learn the building blocks of a simple chatbot
- Create a rule-based chatbot and explore ML-based chatbot extensions

1. What Is a Chatbot?

A **chatbot** is a program that can simulate a conversation with users, either through text or voice.

Chatbots are used in:

- Customer service
- Voice assistants
- Online tutoring
- Entertainment (like character chats)

There are two types of chatbots:

- **Rule-based** – uses decision trees or simple logic
- **AI-based** – uses machine learning or NLP models

2. Building Blocks of a Simple Chatbot

Here are the basic components:

Component	Purpose
Input	Captures the user's question (e.g., "What's your name?")
Processing Logic	Analyzes the question and determines a response
Response	Sends a reply ("I'm RoboChat, your assistant!")

For beginners, we'll start with a **rule-based chatbot**.

3. Let's Build It: Rule-Based Chatbot in Python

You'll need basic Python knowledge for this project.

Step 1: Create a dictionary of responses

python

CopyEdit

```
responses = {
    "hello": "Hi there! How can I help you today?",
    "how are you": "I'm just a bot, but I'm doing great!",
    "what is your name": "I'm RoboChat, your friendly AI assistant!",
    "bye": "Goodbye! Have a nice day!"
}
```

Step 2: Write a simple function to reply

```python
def chatbot():
    while True:
        user_input = input("You: ").lower()
        if user_input in responses:
            print("Bot:", responses[user_input])
        else:
            print("Bot: Sorry, I don't understand that.")
        if user_input == "bye":
            break
chatbot()
```

Learn Coding!
*From our **Coding for Young Minds** books, where you'll build your own mini-AI projects!*

4. How It Works

- The bot waits for input
- It checks if the input matches a keyword
- It replies based on a predefined dictionary
- If it doesn't understand, it shows a fallback message

5. Extending the Chatbot with AI

To build a **machine-learning-based chatbot**, we would:

1. Use **Natural Language Processing (NLP)** to process text
2. Train a model on conversation data
3. Use tools like:
    - NLTK or spaCy for tokenization
    - TF-IDF or word embeddings
    - A classification algorithm or even a small transformer model

Libraries like **Rasa**, **Dialogflow**, and **ChatterBot** are useful for advanced chatbot development.

6. Real-World Chatbot Uses

Industry	Use Case
Healthcare	Symptom checkers (e.g., Babylon Health)
Banking	Balance inquiry, fraud alerts
Retail	Product recommendations, order tracking
Education	Tutoring and FAQs
Travel	Booking and virtual guides

7. Considerations and Limitations

- **Data quality** matters; bad data leads to poor responses
- Users expect **natural conversation**, which is hard to achieve
- **Bias and misinformation** in training data can affect chatbot behavior

Designing a **useful, ethical chatbot** requires careful testing and constant updates.

Reflective Questions

1. What are some chatbot experiences you've had? Were they helpful?
2. How can chatbots enhance learning in schools or improve healthcare?
3. What would your ideal chatbot do?

Chapter 8: Introduction to Computer Vision

Objectives:

- Understand what computer vision is
- Learn how machines “see” and interpret images
- Explore real-world applications and tools used in computer vision

1. What Is Computer Vision?

Computer Vision is a branch of Artificial Intelligence that enables machines to **see, understand, and interpret visual data**, such as images and videos.

It mimics **human sight** by using algorithms and models to extract meaning from visual input.

2. How It Works – Simplified Pipeline

Computer vision systems follow this general process:

1. **Image Input**
   An image is captured or uploaded (e.g., a photo of a cat).
2. **Preprocessing**
   Cleaning and resizing the image so the model can understand it.
3. **Feature Extraction**
   The system identifies patterns: edges, shapes, and textures.

4. **Classification or Detection**
   The model decides: "Is this a cat, dog, or something else?"
   It may also detect **the location of the object** (bounding boxes).

3. Basic Techniques in Computer Vision (CV)

Technique	**Description**
Image Classification	Assign a label to an image (e.g., "banana")
Object Detection	Locate multiple items in an image
Image Segmentation	Separate each pixel by object type
Face Recognition	Identify or verify faces
OCR (Optical Character Recognition)	Detect and read text in images

4. Common Tools and Libraries

Tool	**Use**
OpenCV	Image processing and computer vision
TensorFlow/Keras	Deep learning frameworks that support CV
PyTorch	Deep learning with dynamic computation graphs
MediaPipe	Google's tool for real-time detection (e.g., hands, faces)

Example: Using OpenCV to display and convert an image to grayscale:

```python
CopyEdit
import cv2
image = cv2.imread('cat.jpg')
gray = cv2.cvtColor(image, cv2.COLOR_BGR2GRAY)
cv2.imshow('Grayscale', gray)
cv2.waitKey(0)
cv2.destroyAllWindows()
```

Learn Coding!
*From our **Coding for Young Minds** books, where you'll build your own mini-AI projects!*

5. Real-World Applications

Field	Example
Self-Driving Cars	Detecting lanes, pedestrians, traffic signs
Healthcare	Identifying tumors or X-ray analysis
Agriculture	Monitoring crop health via drone footage
Security	Surveillance and facial recognition
Retail	Smart checkouts and inventory management

6. Challenges in Computer Vision

- **Lighting & Image Quality**: Bad lighting affects accuracy

- **Bias in Datasets**: Poor diversity can cause misidentification
- **Privacy Concerns**: Especially in face recognition and surveillance
- **Real-Time Processing**: Video frames must be processed quickly

7. Mini Case Study: Face Detection

Using Haar Cascades in OpenCV:

python

CopyEdit

```
face_cascade =
cv2.CascadeClassifier('haarcascade_frontalface_default.xml')

img = cv2.imread('group_photo.jpg')

gray = cv2.cvtColor(img, cv2.COLOR_BGR2GRAY)

faces = face_cascade.detectMultiScale(gray, 1.1, 4)

for (x, y, w, h) in faces:

  cv2.rectangle(img, (x, y), (x+w, y+h), (255, 0, 0), 2)

cv2.imshow('Faces found', img)

cv2.waitKey()
```

Learn Coding!
*From our **Coding for Young Minds** books, where you'll build your own mini-AI projects!*

Reflective Questions

1. What would you build with computer vision?
2. Can machines ever truly "see" like humans?
3. How should society regulate face recognition?

Chapter 9: Ethics in AI

Objectives:

- Understand the ethical issues related to AI
- Explore fairness, bias, privacy, and accountability in AI systems
- Learn about responsible AI development and use

1. Why Ethics Matter in AI

Artificial Intelligence can be powerful and transformative, but it also raises important questions about **how** and **when** it should be used.

Ethics in AI is about making sure:

- AI is **fair**
- AI respects **human rights**
- AI is **accountable** and **transparent**

2. Major Ethical Challenges

Ethical Issue	Description
Bias and Fairness	AI may unfairly favor certain groups if trained on biased data.
Transparency	Many AI models (especially deep learning) are black boxes—hard to explain.
Privacy	AI can analyze personal data, raising concerns about surveillance.
Autonomy	AI may make decisions that affect human lives (e.g., healthcare, criminal justice).
Accountability	If an AI makes a harmful decision, who is responsible? The developer? The user?

3. Examples of Ethical Dilemmas

- **Hiring Algorithms**: An AI system filters job applicants. If it's trained on past hires that were mostly men, it might learn to prefer men over equally qualified women.
- **Facial Recognition**: Deployed in public areas for surveillance, it can invade personal privacy and misidentify people, especially those from underrepresented groups.
- **AI in Policing**: Predictive policing tools may increase over-policing in certain neighborhoods based on historical crime data.

4. Fair AI: How Can We Fix It?

Approach	Purpose
Bias Auditing	Check models for unfair patterns
Explainable AI (XAI)	Make model decisions understandable to humans
Privacy by Design	Build systems that protect user data from the start
Diverse Datasets	Include all groups in the training data to prevent bias
Human Oversight	Keep humans in the loop for critical decisions

5. Ethical AI Frameworks and Principles

Many organizations propose ethical AI guidelines, including:

- **Fairness**: No discrimination
- **Accountability**: Someone must be responsible
- **Transparency**: Make models understandable
- **Privacy**: Protect user data
- **Beneficence**: Do more good than harm

Examples:

- **OECD AI Principles**
- **EU AI Act**
- **IEEE Ethically Aligned Design**

6. Voices in AI Ethics

Important contributors:

- **Timnit Gebru** – Researcher focused on bias in large language models and ethical AI
- **Joy Buolamwini** – Founder of the Algorithmic Justice League
- **Kate Crawford** – Author of *Atlas of AI*, exploring AI's impact on society

7. Mini Case Study: AI and Healthcare

AI helps doctors diagnose diseases, but:

- What if the AI is trained mostly on data from one region?
- Could it misdiagnose people from another background?
- Who's liable if the AI is wrong?

This raises issues of **fairness, reliability, and consent**.

8. Discussion Questions

1. Should companies be allowed to use facial recognition in public? Why or why not?
2. How would you design a fair AI system?
3. Who should be responsible if an AI makes a harmful mistake?

Summary

- Ethics in AI ensures the responsible use of technology
- Key concerns include bias, privacy, accountability, and fairness
- Developers and users must work together to create trustworthy AI

Chapter 10: Natural Language Processing (NLP)

Objectives:

- Understand what Natural Language Processing (NLP) is
- Explore how computers understand and generate human language
- Learn about real-world applications of NLP

1. What is NLP?

Natural Language Processing (NLP) is a field of AI that allows computers to:

- Read
- Understand
- Interpret
- Generate **human language**

It's what makes chatbots, voice assistants, and language translators work.

2. Why NLP is Hard for Machines

Human language is messy:

- Words can have **multiple meanings** (e.g., "bat" 🦇 or 🏏?)
- We use **slang, idioms**, and **sarcasm**

- Word **order and grammar** vary across languages
- Context matters a lot

Example:

"I saw her duck."
Did you mean:

- She bent down quickly?
- You saw her pet bird?

3. Core Tasks in NLP

Task	**What It Means**
Tokenization	Breaking text into words or parts
Part-of-speech tagging	Labeling words (noun, verb, adjective)
Named Entity Recognition (NER)	Finding names of people, places, and dates
Sentiment Analysis	Understanding if text is positive or negative
Machine Translation	Translating between languages
Text Generation	Creating human-like text (e.g., ChatGPT)
Speech Recognition	Turning spoken words into text

4. How NLP Works: Step by Step

1. **Input Text** – e.g., "Translate this sentence."
2. **Preprocessing** – Clean and tokenize the text.

3. **Modeling** – Use machine learning (or deep learning) models to understand meaning.
4. **Output** – A response, translation, or classification.

Modern NLP often uses:

- **Transformers** (e.g., BERT, GPT)
- **Word embeddings** (e.g., Word2Vec, GloVe)
- **Attention mechanisms** to focus on relevant parts of the text

5. Examples of NLP in Action

Tool/Platform	Use Case
Siri / Alexa	Understanding voice commands
Google Translate	Translating sentences
Grammarly	Suggesting grammar and tone improvements
ChatGPT	Answering questions and generating text
Spam Filters	Classifying emails as spam or not

6. Real Challenges in NLP

- **Bias in language models**
  (e.g., offensive or gender-stereotyped responses)
- **Low-resource languages**
  (Lack of data makes it hard to build models)
- **Multilingual AI**
  (Training one model to work in many languages)
- **Fake news and misinformation**
  (AI can generate convincing, but false content)

7. Why NLP Matters

NLP is transforming:

- **Customer support**
- **Education**
- **Healthcare**
- **Social media**
- **Journalism**

It's helping people **communicate more effectively, access information, and interact with machines more** naturally.

8. Reflection Questions

1. What NLP tool do you use most in your daily life?
2. Do you trust a chatbot to give you medical or legal advice? Why or why not?
3. What could go wrong if NLP misunderstands something?

Summary

- NLP helps machines read, understand, and generate human language
- It powers tools like chatbots, translation apps, and voice assistants
- NLP still faces challenges with language ambiguity and bias

Chapter 11: AI in the Wild — Robotics and IoT

Objectives:

- Understand how AI powers robotics and the Internet of Things (IoT)
- Explore real-world applications outside of traditional computers
- Recognize how AI connects the physical and digital worlds

1. What Are Robotics and IoT?

- **Robotics** is the field of building machines (robots) that can move, sense, and act in the real world.
- **IoT (Internet of Things)** means everyday physical objects (like fridges, watches, traffic lights) that are connected to the internet and share data.

When AI is added to these, it makes machines **smart and autonomous**.

2. How AI Helps Robots Think

Robots powered by AI can:

- **See** using computer vision
- **Listen** using speech processing
- **Understand** their environment

- **Make decisions** and **plan movements**

Example:

A warehouse robot uses AI to find and pick up the right box, then plan the fastest route to deliver it.

3. How AI Works in IoT Devices

IoT devices gather data from the real world using sensors. AI helps these devices:

- Detect patterns in the data
- Learn from user behavior
- Predict future actions or problems
- Make smart decisions automatically

Example:

A smart thermostat uses AI to learn your daily routine and adjusts the temperature without you needing to touch it.

4. Examples of AI + Robotics & IoT

Use Case	How AI is Used
Smart homes	Lights and appliances learn your habits
Autonomous drones	Navigate through the air using AI vision & GPS
Healthcare robots	Deliver meds, assist with surgeries
Self-driving cars	Recognize signs, pedestrians, and drive safely
Smart farming	Robots detect weeds, check soil health
City traffic systems	Adjust lights based on real-time traffic

5. AI Tools in Robotics & IoT

- **Sensors** – Gather data: light, sound, temperature, motion
- **Edge AI** – AI runs directly on the device, not the cloud
- **Actuators** – Parts that let robots move and perform actions
- **Embedded AI** – AI models built into small smart devices

6. Challenges

- **Safety & reliability** – What if a self-driving car makes a mistake?
- **Security** – IoT devices can be hacked
- **Ethical issues** – Can we trust AI to make life-and-death decisions?
- **Cost** – Building and maintaining smart robots can be expensive

7. Why It Matters

AI in robotics and IoT can:

- Make cities more efficient
- Support aging populations with care robots
- Improve farming and food production
- Enhance disaster response with search-and-rescue drones
- Reduce waste and save energy

8. Reflection Questions

1. Would you trust a robot to help your grandparents?
2. What are some benefits and risks of smart devices in your home?

3. Can you think of a job a robot should never replace?

Summary

- AI helps robots and smart devices act intelligently in the real world
- Robotics + AI = machines that see, move, and decide
- IoT + AI = everyday things that think, learn, and connect
- These technologies are transforming homes, cities, and industries

Chapter 12: AI and Cybersecurity

Objectives:

- Understand how AI is used to protect digital systems
- Learn how AI detects and prevents cyberattacks
- Explore the balance between automation and human oversight in security

1. What Is Cybersecurity?

Cybersecurity is the practice of protecting:

- Computers and servers
- Networks and data
- Applications and systems
From **unauthorized access**, **attacks**, and **damage**.

AI helps **automate**, **predict**, and **respond** to threats faster than humans can.

2. How AI Helps in Cybersecurity

AI can:

- **Detect anomalies** – Spot unusual behavior in a system
- **Predict threats** – Use data to foresee potential attacks
- **Respond quickly** – Shut down or isolate threats before they spread
- **Learn patterns** – Improve over time by recognizing hacker tactics

Example:

AI notices that someone is trying to log into your account from a new location using the wrong password many times. It blocks the login attempt and alerts you.

3. Types of AI Used in Cybersecurity

AI Technique	What It Does
Machine Learning	Learns normal system behavior and flags odd events
Natural Language Processing (NLP)	Reads threat reports, emails, or logs for malicious content
Behavioral Analytics	Understands user habits and detects deviations
Automated Threat Detection	Identifies viruses, ransomware, and phishing attempts

4. Common Threats AI Can Help Prevent

- **Phishing** – Fake emails that trick you into revealing passwords

- **Malware** – Harmful software that damages or steals data
- **DDoS attacks** – Overloading a server to shut it down
- **Insider threats** – When someone inside an organization leaks or misuses data

5. Real-World Use Cases

- Banks use AI to detect fraudulent transactions
- Companies use AI to scan email attachments for viruses
- Government agencies use AI to track national cybersecurity threats
- Cloud services use AI to block access from suspicious IP addresses

6. Challenges of Using AI in Cybersecurity

- **False positives** – AI may block safe users mistakenly
- **Adversarial attacks** – Hackers can try to fool AI systems
- **Bias** – AI models trained on limited data may overlook some threats
- **Dependency** – Overreliance on AI can reduce human vigilance

7. Ethical and Privacy Considerations

- **Surveillance concerns** – Can AI-powered security go too far?
- **Data collection** – AI needs data to learn, but who owns that data?
- **Transparency** – How do we know what the AI is doing?

8. Reflection Questions

1. Would you feel safer knowing AI watches your online activity to keep you safe?
2. Should humans always double-check what AI security systems decide?
3. Can you think of a time when AI might stop a cybercrime before it happens?

Summary

- AI plays a growing role in defending against digital threats
- It detects, prevents, and responds to cyberattacks faster than humans
- However, it must be carefully monitored to avoid errors, bias, and overreach
- Cybersecurity is stronger when AI and humans work together

Chapter 13: AI and Ethics

Objectives:

- Understand what ethics means in the context of AI
- Explore real-world dilemmas where AI decisions affect people
- Discuss fairness, bias, and responsibility in AI systems

What Is AI Ethics?

AI Ethics is the study of **what's right and wrong when building and using AI**. AI can make decisions that impact real lives, so we must think carefully about fairness, privacy, and transparency.

Ethics = Doing the right thing, especially when the choice isn't easy.

Ethical Dilemmas AI Faces

1. **Self-Driving Cars:** If a crash is unavoidable, should the AI protect the passenger or the pedestrian?
2. **Facial Recognition:** What if it works better for some races than others? Is that fair?
3. **Job Automation:** Should companies use AI if it means people lose jobs?

4. **Deepfakes:**
   What if AI is used to create fake videos that spread lies?

Visual Elements

1. **Balancing Scale Illustration:**
   One side labeled "AI Efficiency" and the other side "Fairness & Privacy".
2. **Dilemma Comic Strip:**
   A robot choosing between two ethically difficult paths (e.g., who to help).
3. **Bias Detector Meter**
   Showing low → medium → high levels of bias in a training dataset.
4. **AI Transparency Illustration:**
   A robot showing what it's thinking," why I made this decision"

Key Words

Term	Definition
Ethics	Rules about right and wrong behavior
Bias	When AI unfairly favors or discriminates against someone
Transparency	Explaining how AI makes decisions
Accountability	Making sure people or systems take responsibility for AI decisions
Fairness	Treating people equally and without bias
Consent	Giving permission to use your data or image

Mini Quiz – Check Your Knowledge!

1. Why is ethics important in AI?

a) To make AI more expensive

b) To make AI look cool

c) To ensure AI is fair and safe

2. What does "bias" in AI mean?

a) AI likes spicy food

b) AI treats some groups unfairly based on flawed data

c) AI makes perfect decisions every time

3. True or False:

AI should always be transparent about how it makes decisions.

→ ☐ True ☐ False

4. Name one ethical issue caused by AI:

____________.

5. Which of these is an example of AI lacking transparency?

a) A robot showing its code to the user

b) A chatbot that refuses to explain why it made a choice

c) A news app showing data sources

Class/Group Activity: Ethics Debate

Topic:

"Should facial recognition be used in schools for attendance?"

Assign students into "YES" and "NO" groups, and let them debate, supporting their views with examples and ethical principles.

Chapter 14: The Future of AI

Objectives:

- Explore where AI is heading next
- Understand the potential and risks of future AI technologies
- Spark imagination about how AI could change the world (for better or worse)

What Does the Future Hold?

AI is still in its early stages. Even though it can do amazing things now, it's just getting started. In the future, AI might:

- Work alongside humans in every job
- Help solve big problems like climate change and disease
- Power smart cities that run more efficiently
- Become part of how we live, like AI assistants, tutors, or health trackers

Emerging AI Technologies

Technology	What It Might Do
AGI (Artificial General Intelligence)	Think like a human in many different areas
AI + Robotics	Physical AI that can work in space, disaster zones, or homes
AI in Education	Teach students in personalized ways
AI in Healthcare	Diagnose illnesses faster and more accurately
AI in Environment	Predict natural disasters, manage water, and protect wildlife

Future Challenges to Consider

- **Job Displacement:** More AI means fewer jobs in some fields—how do we prepare?
- **AI Rights:** If AI becomes very smart, should it have rights?
- **Privacy Erosion:** Will AI know too much about us?
- **Superintelligence Risk:** Could AI become too powerful?

"With great power comes great responsibility."
— Popularized by Spider-Man, applies to AI too!

Visual Elements

1. **Timeline Illustration:**
   Showing AI in the past, present, and a speculative future (e.g., flying delivery drones, AI doctors, robot farmers).

2. **Futuristic Cityscape:**
   A glowing city run by AI: self-driving cars, smart waste systems, AI traffic lights.
3. **"Future AI" Concept Bubbles:**
   Students envision different futures with thought bubbles, such as "AI musician," "Robot teammate," and "Climate AI."

New Knowledge Recap

- AI will likely be in **every part of life** in the future.
- **New jobs** will be created even as some old ones disappear.
- We must grow up to be **responsible creators and users** of AI.

Key Words

Term	Definition
AGI	Artificial General Intelligence – AI that can learn and reason like a human
Sustainability	Helping the planet stay healthy and balanced
Ethical Design	Creating technology that's fair and safe for everyone
Technological Singularity	A hypothetical point where AI becomes more intelligent than humans
Automation	Machines doing tasks without human help

Mini Quiz – Check Your Thinking!

1. What does AGI stand for?

a) Advanced Game Intelligence

b) Artificial General Intelligence

c) Automated Government Infrastructure

2. True or False:

The future of AI may include helping fight climate change.

→ ☐ True ☐ False

3. Name one new AI technology that could help healthcare:

____

4. What is one possible risk of future AI?

5. In your opinion, what should humans do to make sure AI is used responsibly?

Reflect & Discuss

- What kind of future do **you** want to live in with AI?
- How can we make sure **everyone** benefits from future AI?

Review & Final Activities: Wrapping Up *Intermediate AI*

What You've Learned

Let's reflect on the journey through *Intermediate AI*. Here are the **big ideas** you've explored:

Key Concepts Recap

Topic	**What You Learned**
What AI Is	AI is about machines that can think, learn, and make decisions
How AI Learns	AI learns from data using algorithms and neural networks
Neural Networks	Inspired by the brain, help AI recognize patterns and solve problems
Data & Bias	The data used to train AI must be fair and diverse
AI in the Real World	AI is used in health, transport, education, entertainment, and more
Ethics & Responsibility	AI must be developed and used in ways that are safe and fair
The Future of AI	AI will continue evolving, shaping the world in ways we're just imagining

Final Activities

1. AI Concept Map

Create a diagram showing how different AI topics are connected—like a web of ideas. Use arrows, keywords, and icons to link terms like "learning," "neural networks," "bias," and "real-world use."

2. Design Your Own AI

Activity:
Invent a new AI system to solve a problem in your school, home, or community.

- What will it do?
- What kind of data will it use?
- What decisions will it help make?
- What are the ethical concerns?

Draw or write a short report about your idea.

3. Debate or Discussion

Discuss one of these questions:

- Should AI be used to grade students' work?
- Can AI replace artists or musicians?
- Should AI be allowed to make life-or-death decisions (like in medicine or war)?

Try to argue both **for** and **against** to understand different views.

4. AI Career Exploration

Look into real careers in AI:

Career	What They Do
Data Scientist	Finds patterns in big data to help solve problems
Machine Learning Engineer	Builds models that help AI learn
AI Ethicist	Thinks about the risks and fairness of AI systems
Robotics Engineer	Builds smart robots that use AI to move and act

Pick one career and research:

- What skills are needed?
- What does their daily work look like?
- Would you enjoy this kind of job?

Final Challenge Quiz

1. What is a neural network inspired by?

a) Spider webs
b) Human brain
c) Satellites

2. Why is data important for AI?

a) AI uses it to learn
b) It makes AI look cool
c) AI eats it

3. What is one danger of AI using biased data?

____

4. Name one place AI is used today:

____

5. What is one responsibility humans have when creating AI?

Reflect: What's Next?

- How would **you** like to be part of the AI future?
- What skills can you learn next?
- Could you help design better, fairer, or more creative AI?

Final Words

Congratulations! You've completed *Intermediate AI*.

Whether you want to build the next great AI tool or be a smart user of tech, remember:

AI is not just for scientists. It's for thinkers, creators, and future leaders like you.

Final Thoughts: You Are Becoming an AI Explorer!

Congratulations, young explorer!
You've now gone beyond the basics and taken your first deep dive into how AI works, how it learns, and how it shapes the world around us.

- You've discovered how AI uses data.
- You've learned about neural networks and how machines spot patterns.
- You've seen that while AI is powerful, humans guide how it's used.

But this is only the beginning!
There's still so much more to explore, create, and imagine as you continue your learning journey.

Curious, responsible thinkers like YOU will build the future of AI. Continue learning, stay curious, and always ask how technology can help people and make the world a better place.

Continue Your AI and Coding Journey!

If you enjoyed *Intermediate AI-Understanding More About How AI Works*, check out these companion books from Nexora Press:

AI Series	**Coding Series**
Fundamentals of AI for Young Minds	Coding for Young Minds
Intermediate AI (this book)	Intermediate Code
Advanced AI (Coming Soon)	Advanced Code (Coming Soon)

Visit **www.nexorapress.com** for full book details and updates.

References & Further Reading

Books and Publications

1. **Mitchell, M.** (2019). *Artificial Intelligence: A Guide for Thinking Humans*. Penguin Books.
2. **Goodfellow, I., Bengio, Y., & Courville, A.** (2016). *Deep Learning*. MIT Press.
3. **Shane, J.** (2019). *You Look Like a Thing and I Love You*. Voracious.
4. **Coeckelbergh, M.** (2020). *AI Ethics*. MIT Press Essential Knowledge Series.

Websites & Learning Platforms

- Teachable Machine (Google) – Create models without code.
- Google AI Hub – AI experiments and tools.
- Code.org: AI for Oceans – Playful AI training.
- Machine Learning for Kids – Learn AI using Scratch or Python.
- MIT Scratch AI Tools – Easy-to-use AI programming extensions.

Articles & Journals

- IBM Cloud Learn Hub – What is AI?
- UNESCO AI & Ethics
- Towards Data Science – Neural Networks Explained

Videos & Channels

- CrashCourse: Artificial Intelligence (YouTube)
- TED-Ed: How Machines Learn
- Google A.I. Experiments

Citation Note:

Where applicable, simplified content and ideas in this book have been inspired by these materials and adapted to suit a youth audience ages 12–16.

Acknowledgments

Special thanks to:

- The curious students, parents, and teachers who inspire this work.
- The many AI researchers, educators, and organizations helping make AI literacy accessible.
- The growing Nexora Press community building the future of ethical technology education.